Six Ways to Think Your Way to Success

BETTER THAN YOU THINK

Drenda Keesee

Better Than You Think
Six Ways to Think Your Way to Success

ISBN: 978-0-9729035-3-0

CONTENTS

INTRODUCTION

"Whether you think you can, or you think you can't, you're right." –Henry Ford

I've discovered that people from all walks of life want a key to success. They want a five-step program that assures them of quick, fail-safe results to make them more popular, beautiful, wealthy, and happy; and the culture is eager to sell it to them at top dollar.

Unfortunately, most of the culture sells *empty promises* of overnight success: get rich quick schemes, fad diets to lose 10 pounds in 10 days, magazines advertising 21 steps to make any man fall in love with you, a lottery ticket to become an overnight millionaire, and many more.... There are real solutions for you, but the culture's gimmicks are not your answer!

Do you think the shade of lipstick or the kinds of shoes you wear are going to make you happy or more successful with men? They might make you feel good for a moment, but when that moment runs out, you'll be searching for new promises to buy into and more temporary happiness to give you a moderately satisfying life. That is why people that rely on material things to give them an identity are always searching and always trying to find more to satisfy themselves.

When people reach the world's standard of success apart from God, they still find themselves depressed, tired, and hurting because their success is founded on the wrong things. They're busy and rundown by the uphill struggle. Families go into hundreds of thousands of dollars of debt to keep up with the Joneses, but it's still not enough. Maybe if they had nicer houses or newer cars, or more money, then they would be happy? But they're not! Since their success is based upon the wrong groundwork, it only magnifies the turmoil on the inside of them and creates more pressures.

Romans 8:6 says, "The mind governed by the flesh is death, but the mind governed by the Spirit is *life* and *peace*" (author's emphasis).

God placed a desire in you for success and happiness. He created you with the innate hunger to find out what you were crafted to do and to succeed at it. That is why those cheap promises of success the culture sells are so appealing—they mimic the promises of God. You were born asking, "Who am I?" and the culture is communicating on hundreds of media platforms, "This is who you are."

It's easy to get caught up in the loudest voice when

it tells you what success should look like and how it should feel. You were designed to look to God for your identity and your answers, not to the culture. As long as you trust the culture to give you something it can't give—happiness, love, value, purpose—you will always be disappointed!

> Do not conform to the pattern of this world, but be transformed by the renewing of your mind. Then you will be able to test and approve what God's will is— His good, pleasing and perfect will. (Romans 12:2)

Your success can't exist apart from God. It starts with God, His Word, and your thoughts. *That is the key.* Success comes from inside of you, from your attitude, from your perspective on life, and works its way out.

> Our thoughts become our WORDS.
> Our words become our ACTIONS.
> Our actions become our HABITS.
> Our habits become our CHARACTER.
> Our character determines our DESTINY.
> > - Gandhi

Your success story begins with a change in your

thoughts—when you learn to think right, you can literally think your way to success!

You may believe that the term "thinking right" is a little vague, unattainable, or even impossible. What do we base right and wrong on anyway? There has been some debate about that, which is why we see the nation in the mess it's in now. But "thinking right" isn't as complicated as it sounds. The word "right'" is a result of righteousness, or the "right way" to do something—God's way. You find righteousness when you seek God. He has given you the amazing gift of salvation, but that is only the beginning! God has made a way for you to live in success. He has given you His Word to help you see the way He sees.

The Creator of the Universe sacrificed His Son for your salvation. Salvation means **welfare, prosperity, deliverance, preservation, health, wholeness, and safety**. All of those things are a part of your inheritance. Jesus paid the price for you to live successfully in every area. If your spirit is alive to God, then salvation (and all that encompasses) is yours!

God has the real fail-safe plan for success in your life. He doesn't rely on empty promises and sales gimmicks.

He has a genuine program to give you real results in your life—results of confidence, beauty, peace, wealth, and fulfillment.

The key to walking in your full potential is to tap into the amazing ability to see life through God's perspective.

In this short easy-to-read book, I will be expounding on this promise and how to apply it to your life. You can think your way to success and see everything God has for you come to pass!

YOUR SUCCESS STORY

STORY

Chapter 1

I remember walking into the kitchen of our 1800's farmhouse, and there was a five-gallon bucket of half dead frogs on our kitchen floor. Yes, dead *frogs*. My husband is a hunter, and he wanted to cook some frog legs. I looked down, and there was one of the frogs, still alive, sliding itself across our kitchen floor. Our house was old, so old that vines were growing through cracks that didn't meet in our windows. We hardly had enough money to take the kids to McDonald's at that time.

I remember how I felt looking at that frog on our kitchen floor. I thought I had failed at life. Somehow that frog was the embodiment of all of my disappointments. We didn't have money, we didn't have an expensive house, and my husband was a *hunter*. I grew up in school thinking that being a hunter was an appalling thing, a label for some sort of redneck that brought dead animals into the house. And there they were, dead frogs in our house.

I had planned on being a successful career woman, not a stay-at-home mom trying to scrape up enough money to pay the bills. My discontentment finally rose to the point where I tried to get a job, to leave everything that

God had called me to, and to return to my metaphorical Egypt. I felt like I was missing out on something.

As I headed to my job interview, I told God, "If this isn't your will, I need you to make it clear to me. I know you don't hit people over the head with a two-by-four, but I'm stubborn, and I give you permission."

God got to my heart through one of my neighbors on the day of my job interview. I was pulling out of our driveway, watching my little toddler with his face pressed against the window waving goodbye to me. As I navigated our long snow-covered driveway in our minivan, the van slid on the ice and I went into the ditch. My husband came running out to help, but I turned my feelings of failure into accusations toward him. I had been trying so hard to be successful, to be a good mom, a good wife, but it wasn't working. Everything I tried seemed to fail.

"You want me to stay here forever! You don't want me to be successful!" I yelled at Gary. I was acting as if he pushed me into the ditch himself!

I struggled as I stubbornly walked our long drive in stilettos over to my neighbor's house and asked to borrow her car. She agreed to let me use it, an old 50's Ford truck with a floor shifter. As I switched the ignition on, the engine sputtered uselessly. I kept trying until the engine flooded, and my eyes filled with tears. I stomped back up to her house to give her the keys, upset.

My neighbor asked, "Drenda, where are you trying to go that's *so* important?"

I told her I was going for a job interview and I was going to meet the president of the company; I was going to be a successful career woman after all. *"I- I- I."*

My neighbor looked at me surprised and exclaimed, "No, you're not! Your husband has a call on his life and you are called to raise your children!"

Bam! I felt the two-by-four.

I went back home and recommitted to invest in my family. I chose to be happy and to trust God with our circumstances, and I was happy because I found renewed purpose in what I was doing. I continued to be a stay-at-home mom while helping my husband with our financial services business, which became very successful. A few years later, we planted a church, eager to share all that we had learned. I am so thankful I didn't let my moment of weakness interfere with God's plans.

I wouldn't change a day of that time in the old farmhouse. Those days *made me*. They taught me some of the most important lessons I have ever learned about success and life. And you know, some days I still drive by that old house and remember the days when an immature, stubborn, young mom had to decide to become a woman of God.

It's easy to get discouraged and give up when situations appear that weren't a part of your plan. Sometimes life feels like a game of whack-a-mole: problem after problem popping up. At first it's manageable, but suddenly problems emerge quicker and in greater quantity—and you become stressed out, overwhelmed, unproductive, and give up.

I am sure you've experienced days like that as well! Monday comes. Someone says something that makes you feel discouraged, or upset, or angry. A difficult situation comes against you, and you're suddenly too busy worrying to spend any time in God's Word or to accomplish anything.

Or maybe you're in a situation like I was in where things haven't gone according to plan, and you feel like giving up.

You can try doing life in your own strength like I did. You can try doing it without God. You can try, but you're not going to get very far. I've learned that dealing with your problems is a lot easier when you invite God into your situation. You are infused with supernatural grace to succeed when you partner with God.

I encounter a lot of people who think going to church is all it means to be a Christian. They think that as long as they mark that off of their weekly to-do list, they are spiritually equipped to handle anything. That is simply not true.

You can go to church on the weekend and get a "spiritual high" and still spend the other six days of the week living in chaos. You have to bring your life alongside the Word of God and develop a personal relationship with God. If you aren't applying those principles to the rest of your week, you aren't reaping the amazing benefits of God's promises or tapping into God's grace for you to succeed!

God wants to help you succeed in *every* area of your

life. When I was raising my five children, there were days I thrived and there were days I was happy I survived. It is so easy to slip into reaction mode as a mom. You have all of these things you want to get done, but instead you spend the whole day reacting to every child's need. I had to stop seeing where my children were at in that moment—diapers, naptimes, feedings—and I saw their futures instead. I saw their potential. I could see the purpose behind my actions, and I could also see how the steps I was taking then would affect my children down the road. I trusted God and did it in His strength, not mine.

The following story is a great illustration of the success story you can tell when you infuse God's power into your circumstances. The names in this story have been changed.

Bill and Stacy moved to Ohio as newlyweds and baby Christians without any money. They lived in their parents' basement for nine months, struggling to get their life started after the move.

Bill was blessed with a job in a Christian environment. His boss, who attends Gary's and my church, Faith Life Church, in New Albany, Ohio, bought them tickets to our marriage conference. They went to that conference and experienced a turning point in their lives. They began attending our church consistently. God began to teach them about marriage, life, and His principles regarding finances, even though they were still broke on paper.

As they welcomed their first child and committed to Stacy being a stay-at-home mother, their finances became very tight. They were living paycheck-to-paycheck and falling further behind on their bills each month. The stress became overwhelming for Bill. He began to slip into depression. He knew that God wanted them to prosper, but he was frustrated.

He came to Gary one weekend and told him that he was having thoughts regarding suicide, which would leave his family a sizable insurance benefit to help them cover the costs of living. That is how hopeless the situation looked!

Bill knew that those thoughts were lies from the enemy, so he came to Gary for help. Gary told him that sometimes when God is trying to give you what you have been asking for, He allows things to become uncomfortable enough that you will be forced to make a change in your life. It was at that point that Bill realized God was moving him toward starting his own business in the insurance industry. He was afraid, but he stepped out in obedience to God.

Bill came and told us what happened after that. They were blessed! Bill made *four times* the gross salary he made at his prior company. He has been able to hire employees, pay off their debt, move from their small townhome to a beautiful new house, purchase a new vehicle, and they had one and a half times more money in the bank than Bill's entire gross salary at his previous company!

Bill and Stacy are so thankful for the complete turnaround God has done in their finances, marriage, and family. Bill says that God has done more than they could ever have imagined! *That* is the kind of success story God wants to produce in your life!

"Now to him who is able to do immeasurably more than all we ask or imagine, according to his power that is at work within us" (Ephesians 3:20).

I stand on this scripture when I pray. I know God is going to do exceedingly abundantly above what I ask or can even imagine. When I ask God for something, I kind of laugh and say, "But God if you want to take it to the next level, I put it in your hands."

When I wanted a deer head to mount in Gary's study, I wanted it to come from our own woods, the land God gave us. I prayed, "God, I'd like it to be a big trophy buck. This is how many antler points I want on the rack, but you could do even more if you want." Gary told me his faith wasn't there for such a big deer. He said he had never seen one even close to that size. I told him, "You believe what you believe for, and I'm going to believe for exceedingly abundantly above what you ask, think, or imagine. I'm decorating your office with this deer head, so I need this!"

He missed an average size buck out in the woods the next day. He began a disappointed walk up to the house. He looked up and in the distance he saw this huge trophy buck. He exclaimed, "There's Drenda's deer! That's Drenda's deer!" Gary pulled up his bow and he shot a long shot. It was way in the distance, but something on the inside of him was excited because he had a promise. He said as soon as he saw that deer that scripture popped in his mind, and he nailed a shot that looked impossible!

He got the deer and he was ecstatic! He came home jumping up and down. I never see Gary more excited than when he sees the Kingdom of God operate in his life, especially when it relates to deer hunting. And that trophy buck looks great in his office! I don't know much about deer, but he said a 26-point deer was a huge deer!

Whatever you believe for, God can do exceedingly abundantly above what you think, ask, or imagine according to His power at work in you. There's a power at work in you, and that power is even greater than your negative thoughts. It's even greater than the negative things you've dealt with in your life, your failure, or your circumstances. You just have to see a promise!

If you can hold on to the promise instead of the problem, you'll renew your mind. You'll keep moving forward into God's things. You're going to see those promises come to pass, and your success story is going to be even *better* than you imagined!

Recognizing success

I once knew an elderly lady who lived through the very tough times of the Great Depression. I would often see her wearing a pair of tattered gloves. I wanted to bless her, so I bought her a new pair and took them to her.

Imagine my shock when she opened the gift, then took me to her dresser, and placed the gloves neatly in the drawer alongside SIX other pairs of brand-new gloves!

She couldn't use or enjoy any of those lovely gloves because her mind was STUCK! Even though she had come *out* of the Great Depression, her mind-set was trapped in survival mode. She couldn't recognize her success, so she couldn't enjoy the benefits of that success!

Is it possible that your success is neatly packed away in a drawer somewhere because of your incorrect thinking? Or that you can't enjoy the benefits or recognize success in your life because you don't know what it looks like?

So tell me. What do you want your success story to look like?

Let's take a look at the apostle Paul. In a lot of ways,

his life was not a picture of success. At least not the "sports car, large house" model of success many honor today. But if we look at Paul's life in the light that over 2,000 years later we are still talking about his life and his legacy, he was one of the most successful men that ever lived.

Paul started off under the name Saul. He murdered Christians for a *living* in the early church as a zealous Jewish Pharisee. That was his full-time job! I believe most people wrote Saul off as too far gone for God. People probably thought God wanted Saul dead! His past was too marred, too dysfunctional, and too sinful for him to change his ways and become a "Christ-follower"! He made some really big mistakes.

After Saul came to know Christ, his transformation was so radical that his former peers were enraged with jealousy and called for his death.

At once he [Saul] began to preach in the synagogues that Jesus is the Son of God. All those who heard him were astonished and asked, "Isn't he the man who raised havoc in Jerusalem among those who call on this name? And hasn't he come here to take them as prisoners to the chief priests?"

After many days had gone by, there was a conspiracy among the Jews to kill him, but Saul learned of their plan. Day and night they kept close watch on the city gates in order to kill him. But his followers took him by night and lowered him in a basket through an opening in the wall.

When he came to Jerusalem, he tried to join the disciples, but they were all afraid of him, not believing that he really was a disciple.

He talked and debated with the Hellenistic Jews, but they tried to kill him. (Acts 9:20-21, 23-26, 29; author's insertion)

When God called the disciple Ananias to share the Gospel with Saul, even *he* protested:

"Lord," Ananias answered, "I have heard many reports about this man and all the harm he has done to your holy people in Jerusalem. And he has come here with authority from the chief priests to arrest all who call on your name."

But the Lord said to Ananias, "Go! This man is my chosen instrument to proclaim my name to the Gentiles and their kings and to the people of Israel." (Acts 9:13-15)

This truly expresses how bad Saul's situation was without God. But even though many people discounted Saul as damaged goods, judged him, and even tried to kill him, God saw the potential for success in Saul, just like He sees the potential for success in you.

Saul was given the name Paul after his conversion, and he began to profoundly change the world for God.

God did *extraordinary* miracles through Paul, so that even handkerchiefs and aprons that had touched him were taken to the sick, and their illnesses were cured and the evil spirits left them. (Acts 19:11-12, author's emphasis)

Paul wrote *thirteen* books in the New Testament. He wrote more of the New Testament than any other one author. Talk about God's restoration! Talk about a success story!

There is no such thing as a hopeless situation with God. People may misjudge you, discount your ability or value, or wrong you—but God sees your potential for success, and He never gives up on you.

Paul went from being a "successful" lawman who killed Christians to a Christian being hunted by lawmen. Still, even when life was miles away from the picture of success, Paul constantly sounded a declaration of joy and victory. Paul said, "We can rejoice, too, when we run into problems and trials, for we know that they help us develop endurance" (Romans 5:3, NLT). Paul gave up temporary status and prestige for a life dedicated to Christ. And in turn he found a success and joy greater than money or fame could offer him.

When you get your priorities right with God, and when you are living successfully according to *God's standard*, then that produces a joy in your life that nothing else can beat. If you can't be happy with where you are at now, then you won't be happy with where you will be at tomorrow. You can only be as successful as your attitude. If you are depending on your success or people's opinions to give you happiness, you will be on an emotional roller coaster. Trust me, I've been there.

Success is not what you have or who others say you are—success is who God says you are. God wants to bless you and give you nice things, but without an understanding of God's perfect love and plan for your life, those things will never satisfy you.

You have to decide what success is to you, both in a spiritual and physical form. When you put goals and reminders in front of you, you can live deliberately. Whether it is getting out of debt or leading 10 people to Christ, it is important to have milestones by which to track your progress.

Take a moment and try this: define your personal success in three very specific points. Write them down and put them somewhere where you will see them daily: on your bathroom mirror, or on your refrigerator door. Start renewing your mind to the picture of success in your life.

Success isn't going to catch you by surprise. It's an intention. It's a decision. It's a mind-set. Be prayerful as you go forward and be aware of what God is speaking to you. Choose to walk this process out with focus and determination. Your life was designed to be a decision, not a reaction. You deserve the life you tolerate, so fight for good things in your life!

Ask yourself:

What do I want my success story to look like?

What is my picture of complete restoration?

What three things have I accomplished this week that are projecting me toward that picture of success?

What are three ways I am already successful and blessed by God?

BUT GOD

Chapter 2

1. LISTEN TO GOD'S VOICE
Overcome your mental blocks and excuses!

You are capable of anything. Matthew 17:20b says,

> "Truly I tell you, if you have faith as small as a mustard seed, you can say to this mountain, 'Move from here to there,' and it will move. *Nothing will be impossible for you*" (author's emphasis).

Isn't that encouraging?

I find for a lot of people that verse isn't as thrilling as it should be. It has no power to them. It has no promise to them. I can't believe that! If you believed what that verse really says, you would be jumping up and down. You would toss this book to the side and run around your house laughing and praising God. No joke!

The reason many people don't react when they read that verse is because they don't believe it. They have it on a plaque on their wall, but they don't even know the revelation that verse has to change their lives. God can't lie. When He says that nothing will be impossible for you, He is *promising* that nothing will be impossible for you. I meet so many people with incredible potential that don't believe that. They can't see all of the amazing things they are capable of or get a vision for their future, because everything is too good for them, too big for them, or too hard for them.

If you try, you can find a million excuses why you can't. How about a reason why you can? Or why you should? In fact, the Bible says that there is no question of "can" and "can't."

"What do you mean, 'If I *can*'? Jesus asked. "Anything is possible if a person believes" (Mark 9:23, NLT, author's emphasis).

"I *can* do all this through him who gives me strength" (Philippians 4:13, author's emphasis).

Your job is not to figure out if you can or can't. Your job is to ask God if you should, and if that's a yes, your job is to say that you will. That's all! Stop letting the question of "Can I?" hold you back and cripple you with doubt.

Dennis and his wife, Nancy, had three beautiful boys: six-year-old twins, Brock and Brayden, and four-year-old Bryce. They didn't feel their family would be complete without a fourth child though—a baby girl.

Nancy became pregnant and miscarried. Nancy's body proceeded to reject and miscarry three more pregnancies for a total of *four* miscarriages in a two-year span. Each time they felt like their faith failed and it became harder to get back up and try again. They reached a point of frustration. They decided they needed to figure out what the problem was and fix it.

Dennis and Nancy went to a specialist to find out what was wrong, but the specialist could not give a clear answer as to why Nancy was miscarrying.

They prayed and asked God to reveal it to them. God showed them two specific things that they needed to deal with, one of which was unforgiveness. They forgave people in their past and decided to step out in faith again because they knew that what God said was all of the evidence they needed.

They started driving an hour and a half each way to attend our church. God sent them on an assignment to figure out how His Kingdom operates and how it could transform their lives. They had to learn to *think* right. Nancy approached me one day, and I came into agreement with her that she would never miscarry again. Shortly after, Nancy became pregnant. She had signs of a miscarriage early on in the pregnancy, but this time she refused to speak a single word of doubt or fear over the baby—and at full-term she gave birth to a beautiful baby girl!

At the same time Dennis and Nancy were standing in faith for their baby girl, they were also having difficulties in their finances. They had struggled financially for the entire duration of their marriage.

Dennis said that they realized insanity is defined as doing the same thing over and over again and expecting different results, so they needed to do something differently if they wanted different results in their finances. Through the leading of the Holy Spirit they found practical wisdom for structuring their finances.

Dennis had been managing a small store of 11 employees at that time. That same business had two locations, and he was managing the smaller one. The general manager of the larger store decided to resign and Dennis was one of three candidates to interview for that job. He was unanimously chosen for the promotion! He now oversees 160 employees and his income has *doubled!*

Dennis and Nancy could have made excuses. They could have said it didn't work before, so there's no point in trying again. But they didn't—and the choice to ignore those excuses and let go of their doubt radically changed their lives.

What *But God* is keeping you from writing your success story?

When we were offered a program on television, we immediately began to look at the cost. We began to think about the expense and the amount of work it required. We began to think about people's eyes on us and that we weren't perfect. We didn't even feel worthy to do it, but we had to see instead that God wanted us to do it. Too many times as believers we ask ourselves, "What is it going to cost me? What price am I going to pay?" Before we know it, we've renewed our minds and talked ourselves out of being bold and courageous.

Your excuses and mental boundaries will hold you back from what God has for you. "*But God*, I can't do that. *But God*, that's impossible. *But God*, it didn't work before." You have to get your *But God* out of the way!

Colonel Sanders's story

I always love the story of Colonel Sanders. He was 62 years old when he looked at his first retirement check. He said, "This ain't gonna cut it!" He pulled out a fried chicken recipe, started a small restaurant, and the rest is history. He didn't hang up his whole destiny just because he was 62 years old. It is never too late to start doing what God has called you to do.

Your excuses and your habits

As for you, you were dead in your transgressions and sins, in which you used to live when you followed the ways of this world and of the ruler of the kingdom of the air, the spirit who is now at work in those who are disobedient. All of us also lived among them at one time, gratifying the cravings of our flesh and following its desires and thoughts. (Ephesians 2:1-3a)

We are used to following the ways of the world. When I dedicated my heart to God, I had more than 18 years of bad habits under my belt that I learned from the world's system. My mind was renewed to the culture, and I still retained those worldly thoughts when I got saved.

As a young woman, I was determined to never get married or have children. I decided I would be a career woman. I thought my success defined me as a person, and so I was always striving and never satisfied. Those were wrong thoughts that I renewed my mind to and God had to work those out of me. It wasn't an easy, overnight process. It was a gradual change I underwent. I had to remind myself to rely on God instead of trying to do everything in my own strength.

God dealt with my heart about the great call it is to be a mother. It was a step to have children, but when I decided to be a stay-at-home mom (what I used to be so against!), I had to renew my mind to God's Word all over again. I had to renew my mind continually to God's Word and clean out those incorrect thoughts!

In Mark 7:13 it says, "Thus you nullify the word of God by your tradition that you have handed down. And you do many things like that."

If we look to traditions or the world's system, we are going to nullify the power of the Word of God. It doesn't matter if you can quote a promise if you don't believe that promise, or if you restrain that promise with your excuses.

I can't choose God's system and the world's system. Every time I do that, I am taking my eyes off of God and I am putting them on the problem. I am not going to receive the promise if I do that!

"Their loyalty is divided between God and the world, and they are unstable in everything they do" (James 1:8, NLT).

The Bible says a double-minded man or woman cannot receive anything from God because they are not in faith. You have to decide if you are going to be problem-focused or promise-focused. Satan wants to tie your hands with problems. He aims to get you in reaction mode so you will not recognize who you are in Christ or the knowledge of your authority over problems.

Now, when I talk about taking authority over problems, I don't mean winning the argument against your husband or anything like that. I mean dealing with the root of the issue: your thoughts. Proverb 23:7 (AMP) says, "For as he thinks in his heart, so is he. As one who reckons, he says to you, eat and drink, yet his heart is not with you [but is grudging the cost]." Satan wants you to rehearse curses in your life. He wants you to renew your mind to your problems and not the promises of God.

Our sinful nature is another thing that tries to control our lives. It is something that feels good to us and has grown familiar. We've renewed our minds to those bad habits in the world's system, and whenever we renew our minds more with the world's system than with God's system, we revert to those habits. You don't want that anymore! You need to stay away from those things that you've broken off of your life by the power of God. We are transformed by what we look to or look at. Make sure you are looking at what God says.

And we all, who with unveiled faces contemplate the Lord's glory, are being transformed into his image with ever-increasing glory, which comes from the Lord, who is the Spirit. (2 Corinthians 3:18)

The Bible says we are being transformed into His image if we look to the Lord. The image we behold is the image we become, so what are you looking at?

Teaming up with God

"Jesus replied, 'What is impossible with man is possible with God'" (Luke 18:27).

God is on your side. He wants to team up with you and to help you go to the next level. He isn't going to ask you to do something that is not ultimately going to bless you. When you team up with God and trust His Word over your excuses and mental boundaries, your life will transform into an amazing display of His goodness.

"But seek first his kingdom and his righteousness, and all these things will be given to you as well" (Matthew 6:33).

People test God and say, "If you take care of this in a week, I'll do it your way. Otherwise I'm going back to my way." That does not work. That is not a relationship with God; that's a contract. If you go into a marriage with that kind of mentality, divorce will always be nipping at your heels. Why? Because nobody is going to do everything exactly the way you would, and neither is God. That doesn't mean that they have failed you or they don't love you. Doing it your way already failed. That's why you needed God in the first place. So it's pointless for you to try to change and manipulate God's perfect plan with your imperfect way of thinking.

Choose to be thankful and to work with God despite your excuses, your previous disappointments, or your current situation. When you commit to being thankful, Satan no longer has a carrot to dangle in front of you. You rip away his pleasure of making you discontent with God.

Satan loves to urge you after material status and temporary happiness, and just when you think you grab them, he rips them away so you will blame God and turn from Him and His perfect methods for you. That is why when you decide to team up with God no matter what He does for you in return, you become invincible in hardships. You disarm the greatest weapons Satan has against you: unhappiness and ingratitude with your situation.

When your circumstances look like evidence that God has failed you, do not turn from Him. God waits until the right time to step in so His impact will be extraordinary. God does not come at your preferred time, when it is most convenient for you, but when your faith is tried so you can't put on a performance. Galatians 6:9 says, "Let us not become weary in doing good, for at the proper time we will reap a harvest if we do not give up."

Stop saying *"But God,"* and determine to tackle every day hand-in-hand with Him according to His perfect will for your life. Stop yourself in the act of making cheap excuses. God already told you that you *can* do it! Focus on what the Word of God points at. That is your evidence. That is your proof. That is enough.

"They received the word with all readiness of mind, and searched the scriptures daily, *whether those things were so*" (Acts 17:11b, KJV, author's emphasis).

God will keep you in perfect peace if you trust in Him (Isaiah 26:3). That's a promise! People will disappoint you, and flesh and blood will disappoint you. If you will keep your mind on Him though, God will never let you down. I challenge you to hope more and to trust God more than you trust disappointment.

HELP!
WHY AM I
DEPRESSED?

Chapter 3

2. THINK POSITIVE!
Get rid of depression, discouragement, and doubt!

Whether you have accomplished an amazing feat or you are at the bottom of the dump, it doesn't mean that depression, doubt, and discouragement will not try to come against you. Even the most "successful" people can struggle with depression. According to a study done by NHANES, antidepressant use does not vary by income status. Success doesn't cure depression, it doesn't cure doubt, and it doesn't cure discouragement. Depression is not a *things* issue: "If I only had, if I only was, if they only were, if I only hadn't … then I would be happy." Depression is a *mind-set* issue!

Connie and Jay ran a prospering business. They were very "successful" and were surrounded with material wealth, but on the inside everything was crumbling.

Jay felt like his marriage was dying, his relationship with their two children was dying, and he was failing at life. There was strife in their marriage. Connie thought that men couldn't be trusted, and Jay thought that women were just there to spend all of your money. They didn't respect each other. When they would lose a business deal, Connie would ask Jay what happened and he would view it as nagging, and that started another fight. Connie and Jay were trying to keep up the appearance that everything was okay because that's what they thought they were supposed to do.

Jay started relying on alcohol. As a teenager, he had struggled with alcohol and drugs and quit. He started drinking again, thinking since he was a Christian and he was a new person in Christ, it wouldn't hurt if he had a beer every once in a while. As problems in their marriage increased, and as stress at work increased, he started drinking more. He quit dealing with his emotions, he quit dealing with the things in his family, and he quit dealing with the problems in their relationship. If there was a problem and Jay felt bad, he knew he could drink until he felt good.

As this started happening, their finances plummeted. Their business plummeted. And this only made Jay want to drink more. He got to the point where he just wanted to escape from life; he hated how he felt and how he was treating the people around him.

When Connie and Jay went through bankruptcy, Connie was angry. She was done with their marriage and she wanted Jay gone. Their daughter was two years old and their son was nine years old. She told Jay to pack up his stuff and leave, but he refused to go.

After Connie's breaking point, she fell into depression. For the next two years, all she could do was sleep. She was too depressed to take care of their kids. Connie shut down.

Jay took over everything—he helped the kids with their homework, he took care of the house—he did *everything*. Jay says that his needs, his wants, his everything had become his mistress. He had put himself first in front of his family and in front of his wife, and he felt so guilty then that he let her be however she needed to be.

The Lord told Connie, "You have a choice: you can divorce him if you want, but that's not my will."

So Connie and Jay came to our church. They were starving for the Word of God in their lives. They were starving for encouragement. They began to learn how

God's Kingdom operates, and God completely *restored* their situation! Connie and Jay have their business again and it is thriving, their marriage is restored, their family has come full circle, and Connie has her joy back!

Connie's situation is not uncommon. Many people allow depression to get a hold in their lives as a result of unresolved issues, but God wants to restore joy, confidence, and vision in their lives.

Did you know 95 percent of depression results from another emotion?

Ninety-five percent of depression is rooted in emotions like anger, disappointment, insecurity, frustration, or pain. When you suppress those emotions and don't overcome those oppressive thoughts with the Word of God, you fall into doubt and discouragement, leading to depression.

Connie and Jay say they're here to tell people, "You can fight, you can argue, give up and sleep for two years, you can be miserable and depressed—but nothing can separate you from the love of God. The moral of our story is that it works. The Kingdom of God works."

Caution: Ice!

I was going to Colorado for a skiing trip with a friend. She was a very experienced skier, and I was, well ... not. I did a last minute crash course lesson the day before (*crash* course is right!), but the skiing hills in Ohio are "slightly" smaller than the skiing mountains in Colorado.

My flight had just arrived in Colorado, and I was having a pity-party over something that happened that week. I let myself slip into wrong thinking.

My friend and I met up at the airport and took our bags to the car. She went back inside to get something, and as I went to put another bag in the car, I slipped on a patch of ice. My head and my elbow slammed against the concrete, and I saw stars!

I didn't tell my friend how badly I had fallen. We went to our accommodations, and when I woke up the next morning my elbow was black and blue. I still went skiing that day (not a great choice), and I fell on my elbow again. The pain got worse, so I went and had it examined. My tendon and my triceps muscle were separated.

I had surgery to reattach the tendon and a supernaturally quick recovery. I was supposed to have a sling on for six months, but after three weeks the doctor said my arm was healing so quickly that I didn't need to wear it. That was only half the battle; afterward I had to fight the fear of reinjuring it.

We all have missed God before. I definitely did that time. But this is so similar to how depression operates in our lives. Something happens that hurts us emotionally— we make a mistake, we slip on the ice, a traumatic situation happens, or we get discouraged. We take on that wound and we build a wall.

There is a difference between emotional healing and building a wall to protect that sore spot. Emotional healing deals with the issue, but it gives it time to heal. It takes baby steps toward recovery, and for a while you may protect that wound in a sling, but you are working toward becoming whole again.

When you build a wall, that wound isn't healing. You actually keep that wound alive when you do that. If I never allowed my arm to heal, that wound would have gotten more and more irritated and the injury more serious.

When you build a wall, you sever and cut something off from your ability to feel emotion. Pain seeks pleasure, which is why people often turn to forms of addiction to anesthetize the pain. There is a certain point where pain seeks to cut off that area of your life. When we experience a trauma that is so painful that we can't deal with it, we can actually cut ourselves off emotionally.

Depression is when we've gotten stuck in that trauma, in that severed place, in that hurt. We keep rehearsing it and protecting it, so we never allow it to heal. Life becomes hopeless, and our vision for it becomes paralyzed. You can't live in that place! Pain is an emotion that we need to be able to feel in order to know when to say no to relationships, situations, and circumstances.

You have to take time to heal, but then you have to go from there. You can't spend your whole life nursing those wounds and protecting them. After my arm was hurt, I couldn't spend my whole life protecting that wound. I had to move on. If I didn't start moving it and stretching it, I would have stunted its healing.

Replacement thinking

When obsessive thoughts come up, you have to replace them with a scripture. When negative thinking comes against you, you have to replace those negative thoughts with positive ones. When problems come, remember the promise.

The culture can medicate you outwardly with antidepressants, but you need the emotional healing that only comes from God. The world isn't equipped to reach you in the places you need reached. The only things the world can do are numb and harden emotions with alcohol, medications, pleasure, and sin. Counseling may give you the ability to cope with things in the soul realm (mind, will, and emotions), but ultimately your true freedom comes from your time in His presence with His Word and prayer.

"The Lord is close to the brokenhearted and saves those who are crushed in spirit" (Psalm 34:18).

People have said to us, "Oh, you and Gary have the Midas touch. Anything you touch just prospers and is blessed." Trust me, it did not use to be that way!

Gary and I spent nine years living hand-to-mouth,

paycheck-to-paycheck. We not only owed thousands to the bank and maxed out our credit there, but we also owed thousands to our relatives.

When we were going through tough times, I put scriptures everywhere: the bathroom, our bedroom, and the kitchen. Why did I do that? I had to remember that I wasn't staying in the wilderness forever. We were going through a hard time, but we were going *through*—we were not staying there.

I was headed to somewhere else, somewhere better. God had a promise for my family and for me. He was taking me somewhere. I was not always going to live in that captivity. I was set free in my spirit, and the Word of God was working on my mind. I was learning how to access the Kingdom inside of me by renewing my mind.

Put scriptures wherever you tend to go when you're in that fogged state of mind. I used to run to the bathroom when I felt depressed or when I was throwing a pity-party. It was my one quiet place, so I put scriptures there.

"Consequently, faith comes from *hearing* the message, and the message is heard through the word about Christ" (Romans 10:17, author's emphasis).

Renew your mind by:

1. Hearing the Word of God

2. Reading the Word of God

3. Speaking the Word of God

Listen to the Word of God. Put on our *Renewing Your Mind* CD, and intentionally meditate on those truths while you are going throughout your day. Read your Bible out loud so you are speaking and hearing the Word of God. Replace your negative thinking with thoughts of the hope and future God has for you!

Changing the picture

It starts with the Word of God. Reading the Word of God without grabbing hold of it isn't enough. Your spirit and your mind have to come into agreement with the Word. They have to come together in agreement, and then come out of your mouth. Out of the abundance of the heart the mouth speaks it (Luke 6:45). That's how you receive the promises of God! That's how you find a new vision for your life!

Quit rehearsing the past. You can't live thinking about what you did yesterday. You have to forgive whomever, whatever, and get a new vision from God that will paint a new picture of hope for your life. You have to believe that God's Word is bigger than your thoughts, your experiences, or what you've been through. God's love has more healing ability than anything that has happened to you!

Put your focus on what is right. I have to say this, and it may sound harsh, but depression results from a focus on self. It is focused on what happened to self. It is focused on protecting self. A depressed person isn't thinking about what God says or thinks about the issue, but rather is thinking about how they feel about the problem. These thoughts become the constant focus until the person shuts themselves off from life and others. They are problem focused, not promise focused.

Depression ultimately can lead to suicide. It is a spirit from the enemy who wants to steal, kill, and destroy. He wants you to think that your life is so worthless that you'd be better off dead. It might have come from a trauma, a pain, or a hurt, but now a spirit has come to try to depress you and oppress you to the point where you want to give up. You have to get free from that spirit of self-centeredness, which is ultimately trying to take you out.

If you keep the same pattern, you're going to get the same result. I see people keep the same negative patterns and they wonder why this year looks like last year, and why they keep spiraling down, even to the point of suicide.

Stay accountable. You need somebody to hold you accountable not to speak negative words over your life. When someone is depressed they think depressive thoughts, they rehearse depressing things, and then they speak negative things over their life. Those negative thoughts become negative words.

You need somebody to hold you accountable when you start rehearsing things that have happened to you and when you start speaking negatively. Take captive every thought and stronghold and subject them to the Word of God.

In the beginning, it might not seem like it is working or you may be tempted to quit. Renew your mind to the new picture, and walk it out. Whether it's a moment of deliverance or months of deliverance, you have to stick with it. You have to get a fresh vision for life. You have to renew your mind morning, day, and night. Take what was pain, what was trauma, what was discouragement, and renew the picture to match God's promises. Jeremiah 29:11 says, "'I know the plans I have for you,' declares the Lord, 'plans to prosper you and not to harm you, plans to give you hope and a future.'"

Let go of self-focused thoughts and hurts, and trust God and His Word. If He says He's going to give you a future and a hope, then that means He is going to give you a hope, and through that hope you are going to find that vision for your future again. You can experience joy, love, and contentment! Life can be fun and fulfilling again! Remember: the image you behold is the image you are becoming.

DATING FEAR AND THE COURAGE TO QUIT

Chapter 4

3. DON'T GIVE A PLACE TO FEAR!
Let go of the restraints of fear and boldly embrace life in fearless abandonment!

Fear has been a worldwide crisis for centuries—facing fears, overcoming fears, succumbing to fears. Man has been in a constant struggle to take back his courage. Stories about people that acted courageously circulate like wildfire. News reports focusing on the woman that stops the burglar or the man that rescues the child from the fire go viral. Why? Why do we love these stories?

Somebody wasn't afraid. Somebody had enough courage to take action in unwelcome circumstances. It astonishes us to see a moment of fearlessness. It *inspires* us to see a moment of fearlessness. We have made an industry of movies and novels based on moments of fearlessness.

Do you remember your first encounter with fear, what it felt like, looked like, and acted like?

Fear doesn't feel *good*. You feel out of sorts and uncomfortable, like somebody is restraining you. You can tell just from that first date that fear is a manipulative control freak. But once you have had that first encounter, there is something that draws you back to fear over and over again.

There is no fear in love. But perfect love drives out fear, because fear has to do with punishment. The one who fears is not made perfect in love. (1 John 4:18)

Fear is a counterfeit of love, so it shouldn't surprise us that our bodies respond to fear a lot like an infatuation. Once we get a little taste, it is harder and harder to pull away. And the more time we spend with fear, the more time it demands. Our minds obsess over it and meditate on it!

When you finished a daunting speech or you tried something outside of your comfort zone—how did it feel? Did you feel free, like a weight was lifted off of you?

I went bungee jumping in New Zealand with my daughter Kirsten, off of the Kawarau Bridge. Kirsten is our youngest daughter, and now that our other four children are married and have moved out of the house, she is the last one at home. Gary and I brought her to New Zealand with us for a conference, and when she saw a sign for bungee jumping, she begged to do it. I knew my husband wouldn't want to go with her, so I reluctantly agreed.

As we reached the top of the Kawarau Bridge, 141 feet up, I started getting a new perspective of what I had agreed to. A river surged beneath the bridge and there was a rock canyon on either side. People going ahead of us let screams escape as they dove headfirst off of the bridge, pulling up moments before their heads touched the water, and bouncing almost all the way back up to the bridge again. Once they were finished bouncing, they dangled over the river until a small boat came to retrieve them and started them on their long climb up flights of stairs.

It was daunting for sure. My adrenaline began to kick in, and when Kirsten was starting to get cold feet, I was the one saying, "We've already come this far, let's do it."

Kirsten agreed and made the jump first.

It was my turn next, and they wrapped my feet together, hooked me to the harness, and told me to climb out on a small diving-board-like platform. Walking with your legs tied together is hard—trying to balance with your legs tied together *while* walking out on a board with no railing, and looking over into a hundred foot drop, was a feat all its own. The worker had to pry my hands off of the bridge railing as I inched my way out. He counted to three, and I jumped.

Those next couple of seconds I was soaring through the air, taking in this gorgeous view, so happy I decided to take that leap of faith. Kirsten and I both had an incredible time, and for the rest of that day we felt like we were on top of the world.

A year later we did a conference in Australia and brought Kirsten along with us. This time she saw a sign for skydiving! Talk about overcoming some fears! Once again, I reluctantly agreed. We were both braver this time, and it didn't take any coaxing to get us out of that plane. We landed safely on the beach, and it was another astounding experience we were thankful we had.

Our latest venture, which we got to do with the family on a business trip we won, was swimming with wild reef sharks and six-to-eight foot lemon sharks in Bora Bora. They were only about a foot away from our feet, yet I was inspired to do this because many, many others had proven it could be done rather safely. I made the choice to face the fear to do it too.

After I jumped off of that bridge in New Zealand, and after I swam with those sharks, I felt fearless. I felt free because I overcame those fears. We were created to *live* in that state of fearlessness. That feeling you get when you go bungee jumping or skydiving, and there is that moment where it feels like you can do anything and you're brave, that's what we're created to *live* in through God's love.

Let me make something very clear right off: *any* relationship you have with fear is an abusive relationship. In a similar way, you can grow codependent on fear and use it as a coping mechanism for situations. *Tolerating* fear, *coping* with fear, and *reacting* to fear are not freedom. Fear and love cannot coexist; fear will never look out for your best interest. Fear tries to replace God's love in your life.

Fear is a counterfeit of love—when we give it a place in our lives, it sets into motion the opposite fruit that God's perfect and unconditional love does. Any relationship with fear is an abusive relationship, and the fruit in your life will reflect that!

Traits of fear

Fear is needy: It doesn't come when you want it, and it doesn't leave when you don't. If you open the door for fear in one area of your life, it will try to work its way into every area of your life.

Fear is controlling: It won't let you do the things you love. It restrains you and holds you back.

Fear is discouraging: It puts you down, always telling you that you can't do it, that you're not good enough, and that you're not capable.

Fear is selfish: It only wants to talk about what you can do for it.

Fear steals: It tells you that you can't have the things that God has already promised you.

Fear is a smooth talker: It manipulates you into justifying your fears.

Fear is bossy: It tells you where to be and when to be there, what to do and what not to do. Fear tells you how to live your life.

Do you recognize any of these traits of fear in your life?

When you look at the traits of fear, you can see that people that operate in these behaviors—manipulation, selfishness, and discouragement—are operating out of fear. Fear doesn't only emulate these traits; fear *produces* these traits in you.

We were created with a desire for love—ultimately that desire is for God's love. Services and businesses prey on our desire for love by selling cuddling and convenient relationships. Online dating websites, tabloid relationship advice, and romantic comedies surge in today's society because our culture is so love starved.

There is only one place that perfect love comes from, and that's from God. He is the only perfect love, because His love doesn't reject us, hurt us, or betray us.

Traits of God's love

> **God's love is unconditional:** He always protects, always trusts, always hopes, and always perseveres.

> **God's love is encouraging:** He revives you with energy and tells you that you *can* do it!

> **God's love is forgiving:** Nothing can separate you from His love. He doesn't keep count of your mistakes. Once you ask for forgiveness, He can't even remember them!

> **God's love gives:** He has promised you more than

enough—more love, more success, more joy, and more of what matters in your life.

God's love is selfless: He knows the desires of your heart and always looks out for your best interest.

God's love never fails: He never lets you down. He never gives up on you.

God's love wins: and that means you do, too!

And God's love is even more! First Corinthians 13:4-7 say,

> Love is patient, love is kind. It does not envy, it does not boast, it is not proud. It does not dishonor others, it is not self-seeking, it is not easily angered, it keeps no record of wrongs. Love does not delight in evil but rejoices with the truth. It always protects, always trusts, always hopes, always perseveres.

Nothing can separate us from the love of God. Without knowing the love of God, we can never experience true freedom from fear. A relationship with fear costs us our freedom, so why do we do so many things in fear, instead of in God's grace?

Fear tells you that you can never live without it, that you're not worthy enough for God's grace, that His grace is not sufficient enough for *all* of your failure, and that God requires too much from you. Fear turns your trust in God back to trusting in your own works.

The fear of man

I used to seek man's opinions and judgments, which caused me to be an approval addict. I lived a life full of the fear of man. I feel like that's something that every one of us deals with. We want to be accepted and we allow that desire to control us. Every fear, in one way or another, arises out of the fear of man. The fear of failure, the fear of rejection, the fear of condemnation, the fear of losing respect or love—those come from the fear of man.

The fear of that rejection produces a trap, and that fear often causes us to deny ourselves what we think is right or wrong, and to compromise our love for God and our desire to obey Him.

The Lord is for me; I will not be afraid. What can man do to me? The Lord is my helper.

Therefore, I will look in triumph on those who hate me. It is better to take refuge in the Lord than to trust in man. (Psalm 118:6-8, HCSB)

Jesus was free from the opinions of men. He wanted to be loved, but trying to win love did not dictate His life. Even when the very people He was going to give His life for hated Him, He continued on the mission that God gave Him. He gave His life for those people. When people attacked Him, He didn't counterattack. Jesus went to the Cross so we wouldn't have to counterattack, and so we wouldn't have to live in performance mode.

When you try to step out as the person God has called you to be, many times you will experience attacks against you, and that is why you *have* to be free from the opinions of men. When we quit bouncing who we are off of everyone else and we switch to God's opinion, then there's freedom.

Did you know that the Bible says to be strong and courageous 365 times? That is once for every day of the year! *That* is how much God urges us to live a life free from fear, walking in His divine purpose for us!

Breaking up with fear

I was giving my grandbaby a bath. I put on my swimsuit and got into our Jacuzzi tub with her, and while she laughed and played, I washed her hair. She was only a year old, and she had been going through a bit of a biting phase as she learned to exert her will. I said, "Do you want to get out of the bathtub?"

"No," she said.

"Do you want to stay in the bathtub?"

"I don't know," she said.

I let her play for a while longer and then I asked her again. When I asked her a second time, she took a bar of soap that was floating in the bathtub and bit into it! That was one way to break that bad habit!

Fear is exactly like that—it is a bad habit that you need to break. Although I wouldn't recommend biting into a bar of soap, washing your mouth and mind out with the Word of God isn't a bad idea.

You were never designed to live a life of fear. God did not give you a spirit that shrinks when difficult situations come. He gave you a spirit that is mighty, self-controlled, and full of courageous love (2 Timothy 1:7). If you are struggling with fear, then you need to switch your mind-set from the world's system to God's system. When you look to God's perfect love and His perfect promises, there is no fear.

Fear is best described by this commonly used acronym:

F: False

E: Evidence

A: Appearing

R: Real

Fear is perverted faith—it's faith in perverse things! It is when you trust in the world's system more than you trust in God's system. I've discovered that many people have faith that bad things will happen to them, but they aren't willing to have faith that good things can happen to them. Hebrews 11:1 says, "Faith is the confidence that what we hope for will actually happen; it gives us assurance about things we cannot see" (NLT).

A great illustration for this is happened to one of my daughters a couple of years back. She was at the house by herself, at night, waiting for us to get home from a meeting. She was in the downstairs area of the house with her dog and her sister's two dogs that she was taking care of for a couple of days.

While she was downstairs, the dogs went into a frenzy of barking and ran to the front door. She heard banging on the door, and when she peered around the corner, she could see the knob jiggling. She grabbed the home phone and called her older sister.

"I think somebody is breaking in," she said. "Stay on the line."

The banging silenced, but the dogs continued to bark. She looked outside an upstairs window, but there wasn't any car outside. She could see a set of footprints in the snow that came around the house to the front door. Another set of footprints went from the front door back around the house.

My son-in-law notified the police, and our oldest son, who lives close by, was over in a matter of minutes.

Tim and the policeman searched the basement, where they thought somebody might have come in, but there was nobody. They went back outside to the footprints, and that is when they realized what happened.

They weren't footprints; they were paw prints—paw prints from the neighbor's large brown lab!

That dog had wandered onto our front porch. Our front door has long windows framing it, and when that dog looked inside, there were three dogs staring back at him. He jumped up on the window and the door, and being such a large dog, his paws hit the doorknob as he jumped. He was trying to find a way inside to get to the other dogs.

It was all an elaborate setup, a masterpiece of smoke screens!

Satan loves to present false evidence to you, and as long as you're operating in fear, you can't discern the truth. He knows how to push your buttons. He knows what to say to get you in fear. Since we have been brought up in a fear-driven culture, that's not hard for him, either.

You have been trained to *react* in fear. Movies, television, music, news reports—they train you how to react to circumstances. When you watch movies that depict the main character reacting in fear to the noises in their house, or to a bad report, you are training your subconscious that the appropriate reaction to those circumstances is fear.

The Bible says that faith comes by hearing the Word of God, and if you put God's Word in your heart then it will produce faith by itself (Romans 10:17). That principle works both ways. Fear comes by hearing and meditating on fearful situations, and if you put stories in your heart that speak contrary to God's promises then it will produce fear.

When false evidence attacks, what rises up in your spirit? How do you respond?

> For the weapons of our warfare are not of the flesh, but divinely powerful for the destruction of fortresses. We are destroying speculations and every lofty thing raised up against the knowledge of God, and we are taking every thought captive to the obedience of Christ. (2 Corinthians 10:4-5, NASB)

Satan has no dominion over you. He has no right to break into your house. Satan uses smoke screens to try and move your faith from God and His promises, to instead put it on perversity and your problems!

You were created to live in fearlessness, excitement, and freedom through God's love. You were created for that kind of perfect love where there is fearless abandonment. It comes from love, from spending time with God, and from setting aside the opinions of men and women.

> The Spirit you received does not make you slaves, so that you live in fear again; rather, the Spirit you received brought about your adoption to sonship. And by Him we cry, "Abba, Father." (Romans 8:15)

Fear tries to make you its slave. But even when the *emotion* of fear comes on you, you don't have to obey it. You can speak to it and take authority over it. You can choose faith in God over fear and the world's system!

Get out of that emotionally abusive relationship and stay out of it. Break up with fear once and for all. And when fear tries to come back, when it tries to talk to you, when it tries to find a place in your life, take authority over it. Run to God's perfect love, because "perfect love casts out fear!"

TOXIC
MIND-SETS

Chapter 5

4. CLEAR OUT TOXIC MIND-SETS!
Clean out those self-destructive mind-sets and bad habits that are dooming you for failure.

I watched my husband once as he mentored a young man who had some financial troubles. The young man began applying the principles that Gary taught him with tremendous success. Gary was his hero—in the beginning.

As the young man started making money, and his paychecks began increasing in size, he could not believe he deserved that kind of money. He couldn't believe he could be successful. Even though he saw the results, his mind-set told him he was destined to be a failure.

He quit working; he grew negative; he grew resentful. He sabotaged his success.

That man ended up turning against Gary. He begrudged Gary's success in business. Not only did he begrudge Gary's success, but he also resented success on all ends. Every boss was a bad guy, every authority in his life a restraint. He lost his job, and after that he went from job to job, from failure to failure. He and his family ended up on welfare.

I had to ask myself why he would self-destruct like that. What makes a man steer toward the ditch? Why would he deliberately set himself up for failure?

After I did some digging, I discovered why. At a young age, this man's father had abandoned him. After that there was something programmed on the inside of him, something that told him he deserved to be abandoned. He thought he deserved failure. He didn't trust anyone who had success and so he sabotaged his own.

Those thoughts told him, "You'll never succeed. You'll never amount to anything. You're not worthy enough to succeed. You're not good enough." Have you ever heard those thoughts before?

The mind loves to be right. If you think you're a failure, then your mind is going to give you a pretty convincing argument. Sometimes you have to tell your mind to be quiet and to listen to your spirit. He couldn't believe that he could be successful, so he proved himself right by sabotaging his success.

He allowed a toxic mind-set from his past to poison his future. It is easy to hold onto the words people have said about us, the times people have sinned against us, and our previous shortcomings and insecurity. Sometimes we don't even realize we are allowing toxic mind-sets to control us!

When Gary and I were newlyweds, I imagined these elaborate, romantic scenarios I wanted. I'd suggest we go on a date, and I would spend that week thinking about how I wanted it to go—the romantic things he would say, the flowers he would surprise me with, and I would picture it like it was something out of a romantic comedy.

Then the date would come. Gary wouldn't say what I had scripted for him in my mind. My hair wouldn't look the way I wanted. I couldn't find anything perfect to wear. I would let a bunch of small things ruin my night! Instead of enjoying that moment for what it was, and realizing the great thing I had, I would get offended with Gary for something he didn't even do. It was so silly! How could he know what *I* wanted him to say, anyway?

That is how toxic mind-sets work, though. They stop you from enjoying life by moving your thoughts from the good things God is doing and the blessing right in front of you, and instead focusing them on toxic lies. And in the end, you're the one that misses out on what God has for you.

Do you need to forgive someone? Are you rehearsing a hurt that you've been through? Are you talking the hurt instead of talking the promise?

It does not matter who got you where you are; what matters is where you are going from here. If God has forgiven you (which He has), you need to choose forgiveness for someone else. You may have had unmet expectations of a person or even of God, but God wants to heal those damaged areas inside of you.

It's not over. God's not finished doing a work in you. Just because you don't see the answer yet doesn't mean it's not coming. "You need to persevere so that when you have done the will of God, you will receive what He has promised" (Hebrews 10:36).

Don't quit! We've been through tough times, but

tough times don't last. The Word of God and the promises of God are eternal. They are always there!

The Bible says that Jesus is the same yesterday, today, forever, and He's no respecter of persons (Hebrews 13:8, Acts 10:34). What He did for Gary and Drenda Keesee, He will do for you. What He promises to any of us is a promise for all of us. You have to believe it. If you don't believe it, you can't receive it. You can't allow past experiences to cause you to develop the wrong pattern of thinking.

The trap of "always" and "never"

Have you ever used these expressions?

"I will *never* get this right."

"I will *never* do anything with my life."

"I could *never* do that."

"I will *always* be a failure."

Watch words like *always* and *never*. They are toxic words! In fact, you should treat them like curse words.

When you look at your husband and say, "You always do this," or, "You never do this," you are cursing him. When you say that somebody will always be bad at this, or somebody will never amount to that, you are declaring that over his or her future. Your words set things into motion, and *always* and *never* are very strong words to set into motion!

Reality check

If your mind is renewed to toxic thoughts, you are carrying around a big red self-destruct button. You can't move forward until you decide to think like God thinks and throw out your toxic thoughts.

What is your reality?

Identify the toxic thoughts that could potentially lead you to self-destruction. Write them down. Start with who people told you that you were or who you should be. We often carry those negative labels from our past with us every day, projecting our past hurts onto our future possibilities.

Identity is a huge stumbling point for many. If you feel unworthy, guilty, ugly, incompetent, insecure, anxious, unlovable, or weak, write those toxic mind-sets down. And don't forget mind-sets like wishing you could change your body or that habit of running to the refrigerator when you're stressed or bored. Anything that does not line up with God's Word, whether it is big or small, has to go!

Write what God thinks about it next to those items. You can reference chapter 9 for power-packed promises and scripture straight from the Bible.

It is easy to skim-read over these principles and these exercises. But if you want the real results of a promise-focused mind, then it is vital that you stay determined. Listen to the voice of the Holy Spirit as you read, and pray for direction and insight as you identify broken areas in your life.

Ask yourself:

Am I sabotaging my relationships because of something I believe?

Am I projecting my past hurts on my future?

Do I have a self-destructive mind-set that is holding me back (gossip, sarcasm, criticalness, perfectionism, fear of failure)?

What is the root of those negative mind-sets?

What does God's Word say about my mind-sets? What are God's promises concerning those behaviors?

.

THE TRUTH
AND
YOUR FREEDOM

Chapter 6

5. GRAB HOLD OF THE TRUTH!
Apply the truth that combats the lies that are holding you back.

The power for unlimited freedom has been given to you. The ability to break through any and every obstacle and move past limits is yours. It's in the truth!

"You will know the truth, and the truth will set you free" (John 8:32, NLT).

It's the truth that sets you free. When you're bound up by your past, you set yourself up to repeat those mistakes. You have to reintroduce your mind to the truth. You have to look at what Jesus says about you!

What does God believe about your situation? Who does He say you are? Who is God and who is He in you?

As long as you base your identity and your actions on what someone said about you, what you did, or on those toxic mind-sets, you can't break off the world's burdens. A person cannot complete you; money cannot complete you; success cannot complete you. You can only find your identity and worth in God. We are all created with a God desire in our spirit, and only God can fill that void and make us complete.

Jennifer's struggle with alcohol started at an early age. She remembers on one of her first days of school in first grade going downstairs and having an ice-cold beer at home. At that point, she already knew her favorite brand of beer and that she liked them ice-cold. Her family moved around to different schools, and she had a hard time making friends. She almost felt like she was living a double life. She put up walls, and one of her escape mechanisms was alcohol. If she couldn't get alcohol, she would use cold medicine or anything she could find to satisfy her cravings. She was looking for a way to escape.

Jennifer's alcohol problem escalated quicker as she got older and went to college. Alcohol was readily available at college. She was an engineering student, working 30-40 hours a week, and she was helping with a lot of organizations. She was running hard, but she also learned that she could play hard. She didn't have a lot of free time, but when she did the first thing she would do was drink and get drunk. That started a pattern of regularly drinking and regularly getting drunk as a way to escape all of the pressure.

She was putting so much stress on herself that she couldn't wind down or sleep without alcohol or chemicals. All of Jennifer's friends drank, so it was easy to disguise how serious the situation was.

Jennifer graduated with her Master's degree and got an amazing job offer. She moved across the country for this job. She was away from family, friends, and all supervision—she was alone except for her "friend" alcohol.

After her first day of work, Jennifer stopped by the store and picked up a three-liter box of wine. She showed up to work on her second day completely hungover! The scary part was that she could still function normally. Nobody noticed, so she started showing up to work hungover every day.

Jennifer was still getting raises and promotions at work. She was still managing people at work. Everything seemed okay, but she started to realize that she couldn't control her need for alcohol. She couldn't stop drinking.

Her addiction was controlling her.

Jennifer confided in a coworker, who helped her get involved in some secular programs. She started going to counseling. She started a 12-step program. They were successful in the fact that they got her sober. But Jennifer was miserable because all that she could think about was alcohol. Every moment, whether it was when she was going to sleep or working, she was thinking about alcohol.

Her performance at work began to suffer. She thought, "If this is the life of a sober person, I don't want it."

One of the days that Jennifer went to her 12-step program, she talked to some people that had been sober for 5-10 years. She asked, "How do you handle the constant cravings?"

They looked at her, slightly surprised. "Oh, they don't ever go away. You just have to learn to live with them."

At that point Jennifer's world ended. It was like a prison sentence. She knew she wasn't strong enough to handle sobriety. She didn't know where to turn because her situation looked hopeless. Jennifer needed freedom, not coping, but *freedom.*

She had a good friend who put her in touch with our ministry. When she called us, she was drunk! That was the only way she would talk to a pastor!

Jennifer made arrangements to come to church that Sunday. She said, "All right, I'm going to give God one last chance, but that's it. If that doesn't work, I'm giving up sobriety because I can't handle it."

You can't buy alcohol before 1:00 p.m. on Sundays in Ohio, so Jennifer went as far as to go to the store Saturday and buy a 30-pack of beer. That way when she would get home from church on Sunday morning, she wouldn't have to wait until after 1:00 p.m. to start drinking again.

Jennifer went to church that Sunday morning. Gary and I prayed with her, but Jennifer says she was really just thinking about the 30-pack of beer in her refrigerator and how quickly she could get home. She didn't believe that God could heal her. In fact, Jennifer believed that God made her an alcoholic and that's how he wanted her to live.

She drove home and thought about what she experienced. She didn't feel any differently.

Jennifer walked into her house and through the kitchen, where she always stopped for her beer—but she didn't stop for that beer. Jennifer remembers standing in the living room, looking at her empty hands, and realizing for the first time she didn't desire alcohol!

As Jennifer plugged into the church and started discovering God's unconditional love for her, she started experiencing emotional healing and true freedom. She started dealing with the root of her problems and the walls she had built. She started to experience emotions. She cried when she hadn't cried in years. Before when Jennifer was angry or upset, she just drank away her emotions. Jennifer was learning to live life again!

Jennifer has been free for over *10 years* now. She is a staff member at our ministry and loves to help others experience the freedom she found through God!

Breaking strongholds

The weapons we fight with are not the weapons of the world. On the contrary, they have divine power to demolish strongholds. We demolish arguments and every pretension that sets itself up against the knowledge of God, and we take captive every thought to make it obedient to Christ. (2 Corinthians 10:4-5)

A stronghold is something you have believed for so long that it becomes the truth in your life. It becomes the truth to you whether it's the truth or not.

If I allow myself to believe a lie, it might as well be the truth, right? Because if I believe I'm ugly, I'm going to act like I'm ugly. If I believe I can't, then I'm not going to try. If I believe that no one will ever love me, I'm not going to project anything lovable to anyone.

We're supposed to overthrow and destroy strongholds. We're supposed to say, "Now wait a minute, I used to believe this, but this is not what the Word says." I measure what I say and what I believe against what God's Word says. I take thoughts captive that do not line up with what the Bible says, and I cast them down.

The world is unprincipled. It's dog-eat-dog out there! The world doesn't fight fair. But we don't live or fight our battles that way—never have and never will. The tools of our trade aren't for marketing or manipulation, but they are for demolishing that entire massively corrupt culture.

We use our powerful God-tools for smashing warped philosophies, tearing down barriers erected against the truth of God, fitting every loose thought and emotion and impulse into the structure of life shaped by Christ. Our tools are ready at hand for clearing the ground of every obstruction and building lives of obedience into maturity. (2 Corinthians 10:3-6, MSG)

"Our tools are ready at hand." What are those tools? One of them is to renew your mind. Another is to pray in the Spirit. You've got to let the Word of God scrub out what has been programmed inside of you. It doesn't matter how long you've had the stronghold in your life; you have the power to overcome through Jesus!

Hindsight is 20/20

I have a lot of people approach me for prayer because they are in a rut of sin. They sin, repent, and repeat. Now, let me make this very clear first—as many times as you fall down, you should *always* get right back up. If you sin, repent right away! If you allow condemnation to grab a hold of you, you are only allowing yourself to drift further from God.

Now that being said, God did not create you to live in a rut of sin. If you're always taking one step forward and one step back, you're not going anywhere. God has given you the grace to overcome your cycle of sin!

The temptations in your life are no different than what others experience. And God is faithful. He will not allow the temptation to be more than you can stand. When you are tempted, he will show you a way out so that you can endure. (1 Corinthians 10:13, NLT)

God has already made a way for you to escape sin, but it requires some effort and wisdom on your part. I have mentored young, unmarried couples that continually fell into sin in their relationships. Their hearts were to do what was right, but in one way or another they kept messing up.

When I asked what boundaries they had established in their relationship, they were speechless. They really hadn't given it much thought! They were spending hours alone together with no accountability. They had no boundaries set up to protect them from themselves. These couples couldn't understand why they were in a cycle of sin, but they were setting themselves up for failure.

God placed Adam and Eve, the first man and woman, on the earth with only one law: Do not eat from the tree of the Knowledge of Good and Evil. They could have so many other wonderful things, but God told them that if they ate from that one tree, it would kill them. That doesn't sound too bad, right? You can eat from the whole buffet, but you can't eat the poison at the end or you'll die. Who is going to race to get a plate of that poison?

I am sure Adam and Eve were not planning on eating from that tree right off. They were probably excited about all that God had provided for them. It was not until they lost sight of what God said and questioned that He was good that they lost their position and provision in the Garden.

It started when Eve talked to the serpent. Eve knew the truth, but she allowed herself to flirt with lies until her mind was renewed to them.

> Now the serpent was more crafty than any of the wild animals the Lord God had made. He said to the woman, "Did God really say, 'You must not eat from any tree in the garden?'" (Genesis 3:1)

Speaking with the serpent opened the door for sin in Eve's life. Allowing voices to speak into her life that were contrary to God's Word cost her significantly.

If there is something or someone in your life that may lead you to temptation or lead you to incorrect thinking, *stay away*. Create boundaries in that relationship. Guard your heart. Just like the Devil did with Adam and Eve, he is going to come to you and say, "Did God really say that?" That is a question you need to be able to answer. If you lose sight of truth, then you lose your position and your provision.

You need to set yourself up for success. If I'm eating healthy, I don't go to the nearest buffet and candy store for lunch every day—that would set me up for failure. Surround yourself with people and messages that are setting you up to succeed. You have to know your strengths and your weaknesses when it comes to sin so you can position yourself for defense against the attacks of the enemy!

EIGHT STEPS
TO PEACE

Chapter 7

6.   WALK IN PEACE
Maintain peace in your life despite disrupting circumstances and conflicts!

1. Watch out for Distractions

On an Easter Sunday morning, I was walking down the sidewalk to my office. I was dressed in my Easter best and I was wearing very high heels. I was walking while sending a quick text to one of my kids. (I know you shouldn't do that!)

I have walked on that sidewalk countless times. I know the way and could probably make the walk with my eyes closed. I wasn't paying attention because I knew the road, but what I didn't anticipate was a tiny little rock along my path.

I lost my balance and immediately started yelling, "Jesus! Jesus!" I twisted my body so I could fall headlong into the grass. I think I gave a new definition to the expression, *holy rollers*!

My perfect morning had now become me lying in the grass with mud on me. Why? Because I was distracted and I stumbled on a little rock! I quickly looked around to see if anyone else had seen me. I was embarrassed and bruised.

It's very easy to walk out life by the traditions that we're used to, and to not keep our eyes on the Word of God. It doesn't take much to get us off. It doesn't take much to cause us to stumble.

The culture is shocking. If you turn on the news, if you look around, you will hear and see things that don't look like what you see in the Word of God. The Bible talks about renewing your mind to the Word of God, but it can also be reversed. You can renew your mind to the shock of the culture.

A lot of believers live a defeated life because they're still living and following the dictates of this world instead of the Word of God. Just like I did on that Easter morning, you start out the day full of promise. You start out thinking it's going to be a great day. And then you come across a small little rock, and before you know it, it's 8:00 or 9:00 in the morning and you have no peace. You have no joy. When you let the small things trip you up, you are renewing your mind to the culture and not the Word of God.

> The fruit of the Spirit is love, joy, peace, patience, kindness, goodness, faithfulness, gentleness and self-control. Against such things there is no law. (Galatians 5:22-23)

That's the fruit of God's Spirit and yet that is not what we see in the world. Many times that is not what we see in our very own lives!

Are you modeling the fruit of the Spirit? Or are you feeding your spirit distractions and allowing the temptation to start stumbling begin?

2. Speak to the Problems

> Then he got into the boat and his disciples followed him. Suddenly a furious storm came up on the lake, so that the waves swept over the boat. But Jesus was sleeping. The disciples went and woke him, saying, "Lord, save us! We're going to drown!"

He replied, "You of little faith, why are you so afraid?" Then He got up and rebuked the winds and the waves, and it was completely calm. (Matthew 8:23-26)

I love the fact that most of Jesus's disciples were professional fishermen. When the disciples were panicking about drowning, they weren't overexaggerating! They had plenty of experience handling storms. They saw this storm and thought it was the end.

Jesus didn't see it that way. The storm didn't intimidate him. In fact, Jesus was sleeping in the boat while the storm raged. Wouldn't it be nice to have such unaffected peace that you could get great sleep even in the midst of a storm?

There is an amazing difference in perspectives here. The disciples were imagining their deaths, crying out for help, and Jesus asked them, "Why are you so afraid?" I wonder how many times we cry out to God for help, certain that we are drowning, and God says, "Why are you so afraid? Don't you have faith in me?"

If Jesus wasn't concerned about the storm, we shouldn't be either.

It is crucial to note that the storm was there while Jesus was on the boat. When He woke up, the storm was still there. The storm didn't quit until Jesus exercised His faith by *opening* His mouth and *telling* it to quit!

We must speak to storms instead of letting them speak to us. What Jesus did is what you and I need to do when we are in the midst of the storms we face in life. We need to know who we are, what we have, and that God protects us. We can stand up in the midst of a storm, and we can rebuke the wind and the waves.

The disciples had completely forgotten who was in the boat with them. They forgot the promises of God, but Jesus was promise-focused. He immediately began to enact the promises of God by speaking the Word of God!

3. See Promises, not Problems

Jesus always saw something different than the rest of His companions. Instead of seeing problems, He saw promises. Jesus knew where His faith was, and in whom He trusted.

When you see a problem that already has a solution,

do you waste time worrying about it? Do you lose sleep over it? Do you grow fearful and anxious over it? No!

But when you don't know there is a solution, you are affected by that problem. When the disciples were on the boat with Jesus and it was storming, they only saw a problem. If they had seen the solution, they wouldn't have reacted in fear.

God has already given you the answers to your problems in His Word and His promises for your life. Living life without taking advantage of God's promises is like taking a test without taking advantage of the study guide. Peace comes with answers. When you know there is already a solution to your problem, there is peace.

Your answers aren't in your problems. Your answers are in the promises of God.

4. Be Bold

When you move off of what the Word says, you become stagnant. You lose vision, grow anxious, fearful, discontent, and ultimately move your trust from God. You see what God says, but then you look at the circumstances.

Boldly fix your eyes on Jesus, and He will make a way.

I want to challenge you to be bold and to be courageous. There are big things inside of you. God's put something special in you that other people need. If you believe anything else, you're listening to the wrong thoughts and the wrong messages.

5. Know the Truth

If there is only one thing that you walk away from this book with, I hope it is the concept of renewing your mind. What you meditate on *will* produce itself in your life.

I can't eat junk food every day without it affecting my health, and sooner or later my waistline. Even when the results don't show up in a physical form for weeks or months, too much junk food is harmful to my body and works behind the scenes. I start to experience symptoms like low energy, fatigue, grumpiness, and sugar cravings. And then, once that junk food has produced its full result, I probably will have a couple of extra pounds weighing me down.

The more junk food you eat, the more junk food you crave—so the process starts all over again.

That is *exactly* how it is spiritually! You feed your spirit garbage, and maybe it doesn't seem to do anything for a couple of weeks. You start to experience symptoms, like wrong thoughts, a white lie, a small compromise, and your flesh starts craving more. And when it has produced its full result, you're deep in sin and you can't remember how you got there.

> But each person is tempted when they are dragged away by their own evil desire and enticed. Then, after desire has conceived, it gives birth to sin; and sin, when it is full-grown, gives birth to death. (James 1:14-15)

You *have* to feed your spirit the truth! If you feed your spirit the world's thoughts and the world's fear, then that is what you are going to get in your life. But, if you feed it the promise of God's perfect peace that surpasses all understanding, then you are going to enjoy the benefit of that!

6. Surround Yourself with Godly People

When filming an episode for the *Drenda* show, I felt led of the Spirit to speak to someone who wanted to commit suicide. I later found out that there was a young lady watching who grew up in a Christian home, but the enemy had begun to get a stronghold in her mind. She thought she was unworthy and worthless. She started to believe that she couldn't be a great wife or mother. Her teenage daughter was going through some rebellion and she felt like a failure as a mother. She began to think that it would be better if she did not live.

She stood in the kitchen washing dishes and laid a knife on her wrist. She thought about slitting her wrists. She was so weighed down by obsessive thoughts; it wouldn't have mattered if someone told her she won a trip to Maui or a million dollars. She was depressed and didn't see anything good in life. She tuned into the *Drenda* program and heard me speaking directly to her situation! God set her free, and she began to renew her mind to the Word of God!

At the same time that this woman was going through depression, I was battling discouragement. I had let myself slip into a doubting mind-set, and I thought, "I can't do this television program. I don't know why I'm on ABC Family. This is just a fluke." I began to rehearse the wrong things myself! I kept thinking about the pressure and the cost, and I renewed my mind to the wrong thoughts.

One day I was headed to a baby shower, and I stopped at a red light. I had to make a decision that weekend whether I was going to continue the next season on ABC Family. They had offered me a contract, and I was struggling to make my decision. I laid my head on the steering wheel, and I started crying out to God. I told God, "I need to hear your voice. I don't know what to do. I don't want to waste time or money; I just want to be obedient to you. Please show me whether I'm supposed to do this or not."

There were 13 women at the baby shower I was attending (only minutes after my breakdown in the car). I knew all of them except one, and she sat across from me. We introduced ourselves and all of us ladies mingled. As the baby shower progressed, this woman burst out, "I'm so sorry I keep staring at you, but you just have to know! You have to know you're my hero!"

I looked at her baffled, too stunned to think or respond. She began to tell me the story of how she was ready to take her life, and how she got freed when she watched the *Drenda* program. I began to cry! She began to cry! It is easy to assume that other people don't need encouragement, but we all need encouragement at times.

You need the body of Christ. You need people that come alongside you and say, "You can do this. I believe in you." That day, I got my answer. It's no coincidence. God will answer you wherever you are at, and He will use the people around you.

7. Decide What You Believe

The only way the devil can stop you from the promise of God is if you believe it. Take self-control and put it to work in your life and say, "No, I'll not believe a lie." You have got to be forceful about this. I'm telling you, this is a fight for your very life. You will become your thoughts. What you behold is what you become. What you believe is what you receive.

Remember, success never catches you by surprise. You can't achieve success by reacting to your circumstances. You have to be deliberate, intentional, and steer toward your goal. If you don't decide what you believe, once again you are like the ship that reacts to the waves—you will end up shipwrecked! Meditate on the Word of God, align yourself with what the Bible says, and establish a firm foundation of what you believe.

8. Believe in Yourself

"So God created mankind in his own image, in the image of God he created them; male and female he created them" (Genesis 1:27). You are made in the image and likeness of God. Let that soak in.

You are not made in the image of the media, or co-workers, or anyone else, but you are made in God's image. There is no higher compliment than that! You are made in His image, you've been translated into the Kingdom of God, and the Kingdom is on the inside of you. Jesus is big on the inside of you. Isn't that awesome? If He can do it, you can too!

Therefore, I urge you brothers in view of God's mercy, to offer your bodies as a living sacrifice holy, pleasing to God—this is your true and proper worship. Do not conform to the pattern of this world, but be transformed by the renewing of your mind. Then you will be able to test and approve what God's will is—his good, pleasing and perfect will. (Romans 12:1-2)

Jesus modeled what's right for you, so model it for the culture. Shock them with peace and confidence that surpasses all understanding. When you see someone sick, or when sickness tries to come against you or a friend, keep your perspective right and see what the Word of God says. Speak the promise and don't focus on the problem. Quit rehearsing the situation!

IN CONTROL
AND POWERFUL

Chapter 8

There was a young woman in Belgium who was born a girl, but her mother wanted a boy. She was rejected as a small child. Her mother said she was ugly and called her names. By the time she was in her early forties, she decided to change her gender because she had loathed herself her entire life. After undergoing the surgery to change genders, she saw herself and thought it was a horrible sight. She called herself a monster. In Belgium, you can be euthanized for emotional pain and she had herself killed.

I cried when I first read this story because I thought, "Where was somebody to tell her the truth?" She needed to know that God created her the way she was and she didn't have to be ashamed of that. The problem was in her mind-set, not her gender identity.

This is why we have to get rooted and established in the Word of God. If we are not rooted in what God says is the truth, we are going to buy into what the culture says. Jesus didn't do that. He defied the culture. He brought answers to the culture. I believe that's what we're called to do as believers.

"'Who has known the mind of the Lord so as to instruct him?' But we have the mind of Christ" (1 Corinthians 2:16).

There are people all around us that are sick. Like this Belgium woman, they are confused and hurt. They are sick in their bodies, but they are also sick in their hearts. Broken hearts create sick minds, and these people end up depressed and discouraged. We have more depression, more hurt people, and more suicides than ever before in history.

Why?

People have departed from the truth and the simplicity of the Gospel. They have renewed their minds to the world, and they believe whatever it is the world tells them. They have believed a lie. And be sure, Satan is behind the lie.

It is our mission to take the truth we have and share it with others. We will be held accountable for how faithful we are with our assignment to reach out to those around us.

How God anointed Jesus of Nazareth with the Holy Spirit and power, and how he went around doing good and healing all who were under the power of the devil, because God was with him (Acts 10:38).

You are anointed to set the captives free. You are anointed to shock the culture—to bring truth, to bring light, to bring peace, and to bring joy!

We are called to bring solutions to hurting people like Jesus did. To have success means nothing if it is used for selfish motives. Matthew 10:8 charges us to, "Heal the sick, raise the dead, cleanse those who have leprosy, drive out demons. [Since] freely you have received; freely give" (author's insertion).

God has given you and me the mission to heal hurting hearts all over the world. That could mean inviting your neighbors to church, supporting ministries financially, or traveling overseas as a missionary—whatever it means to you according to your unique function in the Kingdom, as long as it is sharing the good news of the Gospel with people.

It is my passion to reach women worldwide with real-life solutions. I aid the war on hurting hearts through an international television broadcast, conferences, overseas outreaches, sex-trafficking prevention homes, reaching orphans, and anything I can get my hands on that will help further that cause. That is what God has called me to do, so He gives me the grace and support to accomplish that. Through the partnership of many, our ministries are able to heal hearts in Poland, Moldova, India, Uganda, Albania, Iran, the Philippines, and more through unique outreaches, in addition to the television broadcast. As much as we do, there are still so many more people that need reached.

God wants to reach people so desperately, but He needs willing vessels to use. The need to take care of the hurting is so great right now. When we start supporting one sex-trafficking prevention home, they need to build another. The need is too great for people like you and me to grow complacent and forget that we are here to reach out to others. People need homes to sleep in, food to eat, protection, resources, and the hope-restoring truth of how much God loves them—but they have no way to get it unless somebody is willing to reach out to them. There are more in need than any one person could ever reach alone.

It doesn't take a television crew and an overseas team to make a big impact. You can make an impact wherever you're at with whatever you have. I receive incredible stories day-in and day-out of lives transformed by God that started with an invite to church. This testimony paints a great picture of the hurt and desperation that could be all around you, and how someone like you, with a simple invitation to church or the message of God's love, can radically change the situation.

A few years ago I came into contact with the powerful love of God. The Holy Spirit came rushing into my life and began to do a quick work in my family and me. My mind and heart were transforming, and God was healing years of loss, brokenness, sickness, and pain rapidly.

I grew up in a violent home, with an abusive, alcohol and drug addicted father. By the time I was six-years-old, I was fatherless. My dad died in an alcohol-related accident when he was 23 years old. My young widowed mother was in one bad relationship after another and spent years battling addiction. She sent my brother and me to live with relatives for a couple of years, which left me feeling abandoned.

Once we returned to live with her, we were right back in the violence and alcohol-controlled environment. There was more tragedy in the family as my young uncle also died an alcohol related death, and then a few years later my two teenage cousins died in a car accident.

It was a painful time. I was starving for love and attention. I felt broken, worthless, trashy, and of no value. I didn't think I would ever do anything good in life. I acted out as a teenager, having sexual relations and drinking by the age of 14. I was a single mother myself by the age of 19. I got married and brought my mess and brokenness right into an unsuspecting man's life. We immediately began a family.

Our family had tried church over the years. We had tried the God thing, and it hadn't "worked" for us. As time passed, kids who had easily said "yes" to Jesus had become kids that were struggling to believe there was a God. We found ourselves out of church and heading down a slippery slope.

And now alcohol had regained control over me, and I was making poor decisions personally and for my family. I would preach to my kids about doing the right thing, yet what they were seeing me do was not at all what I was preaching to them. I just kept laying down the law with my words and living the opposite of what I was laying down. Our kids didn't respect us, didn't trust us, and didn't want to be around us. They simply were obedient out of fear, or they just learned to "behave" when we were looking.

This was going on for about a year that we were totally out of church. We kept getting invitations to your church. It was like five different invites and all different people, and over half of them we didn't know at all.

We finally got the message and just decided to go so that we could get it out of the way and be done with it. I was convinced we wouldn't like it. Three years ago, in the cold month of February, we took our family to Faith Life Church. We sat ourselves in the back and planned to escape quickly. We were about to have an encounter with the Living God and have our lives transformed.

God did a rapid work in our family, and the timing was critical. I don't even like to consider what we would have gone through had we not encountered His love and the truth that set our family free.

Through the Holy Spirit, the Word of God, and the examples of love, family, and servanthood at Faith Life Church, our lives have been renewed and restored!

When I came to FLC, I was on medications for thyroid disease, had been taking anti-anxiety drugs, acid reflux [drugs], and allergy medicines. I am totally medication free today, and I feel amazing! God has healed my body. I truly believe that I was sin-sick and that stress was making me sick. I was also a binge drinker when I arrived at FLC. I wouldn't drink necessarily every day, but when I would drink it was until I couldn't drink anymore. It was in extreme excess. I smoked cigarettes, too. I was quickly freed from those addictions when I gave them to God.

This was all within the first year of being at FLC. My husband was also freed from cigarettes. He also has been freed and come off of blood pressure medication and anti-anxiety drugs.

Before God I battled depression, alcoholism, and extreme relationship dysfunction. I blamed, I ran, and I cheated. I devalued the life of others. I took the lives of two innocent children in the womb and abandoned my husband and kids in many ways. I attempted suicide and was on antidepressants. I have been healed from a past of abuse, addiction, pain, loss, abandonment, rejection, and the heartbreak of abortion. My marriage and family have been restored, and God is additionally rebuilding relationships that had been broken outside of my immediate family.

I am learning to love and that I am loved. I am seeing the generational curses that have been cycling in my family be cut off and watching as God does this great work in the lives of our kids.

As I write this tonight, I am cuddled happily with my husband of 18 years and our two youngest kids, while the three oldest are at youth group being leaders amongst their peers and serving God. They LOVE God! They are passionate about Him, and they are BELIEVERS!

We have a lot of living left, and through God's healing touch and revealed truth and powerful Spirit we will spend our days proclaiming the works of the Lord! God has healed and restored it all! He has mended my broken heart and brought healing to our whole family. There is nothing my God cannot do!

God is SO good! And He wants to use you to change the culture!

You are called to shock the culture. You are called to have your mind so renewed that when you step out the world sees something different in you. They shouldn't see a weak, anemic Christian, because the Blood of Jesus is not anemic. The Blood of Jesus is powerful! That is what courses through your veins!

You have been translated out of the kingdom of darkness and into the Kingdom that produces life. Life flows through your body and it produces strength, energy, and everything that we see in Jesus. Keep your mind focused on the Word of God and sharing the glory of God with others.

> Finally, brothers and sisters, whatever is true, whatever is noble, whatever is right, whatever is pure, whatever is lovely, whatever is admirable— if anything is excellent or praiseworthy—think about such things. (Philippians 4:8)

Think on what God says. It is going to take an effort, but it is well worth it in the end. You have to fight for truth in your family, in your relationships, and in your life. If you don't fight for the truth, you will cope with the lies.

Continuously restore your mind by:

1. Hearing the Word of God

2. Reading the Word of God

3. Speaking the Word of God

Remember that God loves you. Remember that He WANTS you to win in life! He has an amazing plan for your life that goes beyond anything you can think or imagine.

There are no hopeless situations.

Be strong and courageous, do not be afraid nor dismayed for the Lord your God is with you wherever you go. (Joshua 1:9b)

You've got to renew your mind to the fact that no matter what, God loves you. He's never going to forsake you. He's always with you. He's with you wherever you go so you can shock the culture like Jesus did. Instead of being renewed to their pain and their dysfunction, you can stand up in the face of adversity and put forth a promise. That promise will bring you into victory! It will give you courage to speak up when you need to speak up and the courage to say, "I believe God, no matter what the circumstances say!"

In God, ALL things are "yes" and "amen." You can succeed, not just by the world's fickle standards, but you can fulfill the amazing calling that God has for you.

I pray that you grasp how wide and long and deep God's love for you is! You've got to know this love that surpasses knowledge. It's better than any person. It won't let you down. "God demonstrates his own love for us in this: while we were still sinners Christ died for us" (Romans 5:8).

This is how love is made complete among us so that we will have confidence on the day of judgment: In this world we are like Jesus. (1 John 4:17)

Let that go through your mind for a minute. The Bible says as He is, so are we in this world. God has given us everything we need to live our lives full of passion and life! God has given us everything we need to overcome situations, to live lives of success in every area, and to share the truth with the world!

Prayer

As we reach the end of this book, I encourage you to meditate on the words of this prayer. Speak them out loud and begin to enact the power of joy in your life:

Father, I thank you, in the name of Jesus, that I overcome by the Blood of the Lamb and the word of my testimony as I believe your promises. I thank you that every stronghold that's held me captive, every lie of the enemy, is broken right now. I release lies from my life that came from my parents or people in my past that said I'd never be anything. I break off lies from relationships that said I couldn't be loved. I receive your love, Father, and I give love! I break off lies of the enemy that say that I can never have financial success or that I'll never be able to rise up and do something great. I am seated with Christ in heavenly places! Right now, I take the situations I'm dealing with and I cast them down. They are under my feet because Jesus lives inside of me! Every power, every principality, every might, every dominion, every ruler, every authority in high places has to bow to the name of Jesus!

Thank you, Lord, for teaming up with me and empowering me to live a successful and joyful life!

Amen!

EVERYDAY PROMISES FOR YOUR LIFE

Chapter 9

The Bible contains *thousands* of powerful promises that can transform every area of your life. This is a topical reference of only a limited amount of those truths. Pair this with our *Renewing Your Mind* CD and position your thoughts in agreement with God's promises for you!

I can overcome addictions

"If you hold to my teaching, you are really my disciples. Then you will know the truth, and the truth will set you free" (John 8:31b-32).

I can be free from strongholds

"The weapons we fight with are not the weapons of the world. On the contrary, they have divine power to demolish strongholds. We demolish arguments and every pretension that sets itself up against the knowledge of God, and we take captive every thought to make it obedient to Christ" (2 Corinthians 10:4-5).

I can overcome temptation

"The temptations in your life are no different from what others experience. And God is faithful. He will not allow the temptation to be more than you can stand. When you are tempted, he will show you a way out so that you can endure" (1 Corinthians 10:13, NLT).

I can overcome my sin

"So I say, walk by the Spirit, and you will not gratify the desires of the flesh" (Galatians 5:16).

A life of sin aims for destruction

"What benefit did you reap at that time from the things you are now ashamed of? Those things result in death" (Romans 6:21)! "But each person is tempted when they are dragged away by their own evil desire and enticed. Then, after desire has conceived, it gives birth to sin; and sin, when it is full-grown, gives birth to death" (James 1:14-15).

My sins are not too great for God to forgive

"'Come now, let us settle the matter,' says the Lord. 'Though your sins are like scarlet, they shall be as white as snow; though they are red as crimson, they shall be like wool'" (Isaiah 1:18). "For I will forgive their wickedness and will remember their sins no more" (Hebrews 8:12). "In your love you kept me from the pit of destruction; you have put all my sins behind your back" (Isaiah 38:17b).

God's love will never fail me

"God remembered us when we were down, His love never quits. Rescued us from the trampling boot, His love never quits. Takes care of everyone in time of need. His love never quits. Thank God, who did it all! His love never quits! (Psalm 136:23-26, MSG). "Do not be afraid or discouraged, for the Lord will personally go ahead of you. He will be with you; he will neither fail you nor abandon you" (Deuteronomy 31:6).

I have peace

"I have told you these things, so that in me you may have peace. In this world you will have trouble. But take heart! I have overcome the world" (John 16:33). "Peace I leave with you; my peace I give you. I do not give to you as the world gives. Do not let your hearts be troubled and do not be afraid" (John 14:27).

I am fearless

"For God has not given us a spirit of fear, but of power and of love and of a sound mind" (1 Timothy 1:7, NKJV). "Say to those with fearful hearts, 'Be strong, and do not fear, for your God is coming to destroy your enemies. He is coming to save you.'" (Isaiah 35:4, NLT).

I do not fear harm

"But all who listen to me will live in peace, untroubled by fear of harm" (Proverb 1:33, NLT).

I am bold

"Since we have such a hope, we are very bold" (2 Corinthians 3:12, ESV). "The wicked flee when no one pursues, but the righteous are bold as a lion" (Proverb 28:1, NKJV).

I am forgiven

"If we confess our sins, he is faithful and just and will forgive us our sins and purify us from all unrighteousness" (1 John 1:9).

I have a hope and a future

"'For I know the plans I have for you,' declares the Lord, 'plans to prosper you and not to harm you, plans to give you hope and a future'" (Jeremiah 29:11).

God has a plan for my life

"For we are God's handiwork, created in Christ Jesus to do good works, which God prepared in advance for us to do" (Ephesians 2:10).

God hears and answers my prayers

"And I will do whatever you ask in my name, so that the Father may be glorified in the Son. You may ask me for anything in my name, and I will do it" (John 14:13-14).

I prosper

"And my God will meet all your needs according to the riches of his glory in Christ Jesus" (Philippians 4:19). "Give, and you will receive. Your gift will return to you in full—pressed down, shaken together to make room for more, running over, and poured into your lap. The amount you give will determine the amount you get back" (Luke 6:38, NLT).

I am successful

"Commit your actions to the Lord, and your plans will succeed" (Proverb 16:3). "Take delight in the Lord, and he will give you the desires of your heart" (Psalm 37:4).

I have joy

"But the fruit of the Spirit is love, joy, peace, patience, kindness, goodness, faithfulness" (Galatians 5:22, ESV).

I am beautiful

"I praise you because I am fearfully and wonderfully made; your works are wonderful, I know that full well" (Psalm 139:14).

I am confident

"For the Lord will be your confidence and will keep your foot from being caught" (Proverb 3:26, ESV). "Don't be afraid, for I am with you. Don't be discouraged, for I am your God. I will strengthen you and help you. I will hold you up with my victorious right hand." (Isaiah 41:10, NLT).

I am protected

"The Lord will keep you from all harm—he will watch over your life" (Psalm 121:7).

I can trust God

"And we know that for those who love God all things work together for good, for those who are called according to his purpose" (Romans 8:28, ESV).

I am healed

"Surely he took up our pain and bore our suffering, yet we considered him punished by God, stricken by him, and afflicted. But he was pierced for our transgressions, he was crushed for our iniquities; the punishment that brought us peace was on him, and by his wounds we are healed" (Isaiah 53:4-5).

I am not alone

"For the Lord your God will be with you, wherever you go" (Joshua 1:9b).

God will never leave me

"I will never leave you or forsake you" (Hebrews 13:5, NKJV).

My youth is renewed

"Who satisfies your desires with good things so that your youth is renewed like the eagle's" (Psalm 103:5).

I have energy

"He gives power to the weak and strength to the powerless. Even youth will become weak and tired, and young men will fall in exhaustion. But those who trust in the Lord will find new strength. They will soar high on wings like eagles. They will run and not grow weary. They will walk and not faint" (Isaiah 40:29-31, NLT).

My past does not command my future

"This means that anyone who belongs to Christ has become a new person. The old life is gone; a new life has begun" (2 Corinthians 5:17, NLT)!

I will reap what I sow

"Don't be misled—you cannot mock the justice of God. You will always harvest what you plant" (Galatians 6:7, NLT).

I am loved

"But God demonstrates his own love for us in this: While we were still sinners, Christ died for us" (Romans 5:8).

God is good

"Give thanks to the Lord, for he is good. His love endures forever" (Psalm 136:1).

God is faithful to me

"So the Lord must wait for you to come to him so he can show you his love and compassion. For the Lord is a faithful God. Blessed are those who wait for his help" (Isaiah 30:18, NLT).

God is enough

"But he said to me, 'My grace is sufficient for you, for my power is made perfect in weakness.' Therefore I will boast all the more gladly about my weaknesses, so that Christ's power may rest on me" (2 Corinthians 12:9).

I can do it

"'If you can?' said Jesus. 'Everything is possible for one who believes'" (Mark 9:23). "Jesus looked at them and said, 'With man this is impossible, but with God all things are possible'" (Matthew 19:26).

I don't have to perform for God's love

"For I am convinced that neither death nor life, neither angels nor demons, neither the present nor the future, nor any powers, neither height nor depth, nor anything else in all creation, will be able to separate us from the love of God that is in Christ Jesus our Lord" (Romans 8:38-39). "Salvation is not a reward for the good things we have done, so none of us can boast about it" (Ephesians 2:9, NLT).

I have the victory

"But thanks be to God! He gives us the victory through our Lord Jesus Christ" (1 Corinthians 15:57). "For everyone born of God overcomes the world. This is the victory that has overcome the world, even our faith" (1 John 5:4).

I have a comforter and counselor in the Holy Spirit

"But the Comforter (Counselor, Helper, Intercessor, Advocate, Strengthener, Standby), the Holy Spirit, Whom the Father will send in My name [in My place, to represent Me and act on My behalf] . . . will cause you to recall (will remind you of, bring to your remembrance) everything I have told you" (John 14:26, AMP).

I have access to God's grace

"Through whom we have gained access by faith into this grace in which we now stand. And we boast in the hope of the glory of God" (Romans 5:2).

God knows about my situation

"Do not be like them, for your Father knows what you need before you ask him" (Matthew 6:8).

I will live a long life

"For through wisdom your days will be many, and years will be added to your life" (Proverb 9:11).